ISBN 978-0-259-29261-6
PIBN 10005791

English
Français
Deutsche
Italiano
Español
Português

www.forgottenbooks.com

Mythology Photography **Fiction**
Fishing Christianity **Art** Cooking
Essays Buddhism Freemasonry
Medicine **Biology** Music **Ancient**
Egypt Evolution Carpentry Physics
Dance Geology **Mathematics** Fitness
Shakespeare **Folklore** Yoga Marketing
Confidence Immortality Biographies
Poetry **Psychology** Witchcraft
Electronics Chemistry History **Law**
Accounting **Philosophy** Anthropology
Alchemy Drama Quantum Mechanics
Atheism Sexual Health **Ancient History**
Entrepreneurship Languages Sport
Paleontology Needlework Islam
Metaphysics Investment Archaeology
Parenting Statistics Criminology
Motivational

CULTURE AND REFORM

BY

ANNA ROBERTSON BROWN, Ph.D.

AUTHOR OF "WHAT IS WORTH WHILE?" AND
"THE VICTORY OF OUR FAITH"

NINTH THOUSAND

NEW YORK
THOMAS Y. CROWELL & COMPANY
PUBLISHERS

CULTURE AND REFORM.

" *Of this thing, however, be certain : wouldst thou plant for Eternity, then plant into the deep infinite faculties of man.*"

CARLYLE.

CULTURE AND REFORM.

THE world-aspect changes. Society is not the same to-day that it was yesterday, and to-morrow it will have assumed new forms. The world-aspect not only changes, it shows progress. The race is grander now than it was in years gone by. The soul of man aspires. It looks out on future ages with a large and joyous hope.

When we look at human progress we see that it has come about along three lines. The intellect has become more keen. We know more than of old. Within a few years we have had steam-power, the telegraph, the phonograph, the trolley, and the Rœntgen ray. The heart has been enlarged. We know daily more of true and faithful love. We are kinder than we were a thousand years ago. We provide more efficiently for the weak, the downtrodden, the ignorant, the maimed, and poor. The moral ideal has risen. World-virtue is more triumphant. The race-will is firmer, and chooses better things than ever it chose before.

Under all the varying aspects of history, there have been two chief social forces at work : I call them Culture and Reform. From generation to generation they two, a dual fate, have moulded man.

Culture is conservative. It represents the established condition of a civilization,—the height of its refinement, moral standing, and intellectual repose. It maintains dynasties, laws, schools, social codes, and conventional faith. It is slow to act, hard to arouse, convince, or turn. Reform is revolutionary. It represents dynamic instincts and powers. It works to change the old order, and to pull a civilization out of its present state into new conditions, freer and better than the old. Reform includes wars, rebellions, and dissent. It is led by moral autocrats. It is headstrong, impetuous, determined, radical. Culture stands for the humane, æsthetic side of life ; reform, for the unresting tragic. Working together upon primitive man, they have built of the past this to-day in which we live.

It is a very perplexing To-day. Its many problems vex and embarrass the soul. It shifts so continually beneath our feet that we feel the social basis to be of wind-blown sand. How shall we build our lives ? Where is there rock, if any ? Where shall energy go ? What shall be our aim ? These questions press heavily upon the heart of every one who would be a helper in the world. Time is precious, and so short ! Almost before we grasp it, it is gone. While we are making up our minds, we die.

The problem of life meets each of us squarely. Whatever else we do, we cannot escape the roar of the hurricane which is just now in the air. Our times are exceptional and transitional. The world is moving into new conditions, and we are being hurled with it. Change is imperious; it brings a new environment, and demands a new ideal. What is our part in the onward movement? Which forward call shall we obey?

Among the chief issues before us to-day are those concerning the Home, Temperance, the Sabbath, Missions, Social Purity, Labor and Capital, Legislative and Municipal Honor, Race-adjustment, Charities and Correction, and International Arbitration..

These are large questions. They cannot be settled in a day. We can only say a word about culture and reform as affecting such vital problems. It is social guidance that we need. We need laws of world-conduct, — something under which we can range our individual lives. The worth of individual effort, we see clearly, is in direct proportion to its harmony with some universal truth. What shall this truth be? Let us inquire what the true basis of reform should be, on which all varying phases may be safely founded; in what spirit reform should work, and for what final end. Also what culture can do for reform, so that both working together may in reality and truth uplift, inspire, and guide the race.

I. WHAT TRUE REFORM MUST DO.

Reform must strike deep. It must be ethical, adequate, and permanent. It cannot scratch the surface of wrong-doing and succeed. It must lay hold of world-conditions, aspirations, and demands. It must appeal to vital needs: it must have a godlike grip on life.

From all time there have been certain things that earth has battled with in trying to free her children from the dominion of the temporal, and lift them to the things which are eternal. For instance, there are the marked forms of primitive strife,—the clash of caste, the clash of sex, and the clash of will.

Caste-hatred has its roots in envy, selfishness, and pride. Cain and Abel belonged to different planes of life; and Cain hated the brother above him, and slew him because of his higher rank with God. The Cain-and-Abel struggle has gone on from that day until this. The world has passed through fierce seasons of revolution, unrest, and social discontent. Class is now drawn up against class, and there is mutual antagonism between the two. What has brought all this about? Who has broken social law? The present conflict between capital and labor is but a superficial phase. The primitive strife lies far below this outward sign of it. If reform works only on the capital-and-labor aspect, it will be shallow and incomplete. Dividing the world into two great classes, we see the ruling and the ruled. One class has been overbearing, arrogant, and unjust; the other has been unreasonable and revengeful. Both have been selfish. We cannot rid ourselves of this social conflict by mere human law, however just and wise. Law may hold back a man's hand from robbery, oppression, or murder, but it will not take sullenness, dislike, tyranny, jealousy, or hatred from his heart. It is from the heart that caste-hatred springs. Reform must get at the heart if it will make two opposing castes endure each other. To make them work harmoniously together, a great change must be wrought in class-nature.

The clash of sex is also primitive. Adam was a telltale, and blamed Eve. We have not yet found out exactly where the man belongs, and where the woman, in an ideal state. It is in our day that this strange combat is, so far, at its height. I sometimes wonder if our age will go down in history as the age in which the race of woman was at war with the race of man. Looking over the literature of our times, it seems as if this might be the case. What is the meaning of this strife? What will end it? From what source is enlightenment, is adjustment, to come?

Many other social troubles may be summed up under the third phrase, — clash of will. No matter what our individual creed may be, we do not live long in the world without finding out that, plan as we may, choose as we may, there is somewhere in the universe a will other than our own. Things do not turn out as we wish. Our plans are frustrated, our hopes are dispelled; we meet disappointment and mysterious perplexity and contradictions in our temperament, friendships, experiences, and career. Sorrow lays hold on us; and grief, pain, and loss are round about our way.

What does it all mean? Why cannot we do as
we please? We have freedom of will, but our
action is not free. What hinders us from carrying
out our own decrees?

Reform must find some way of settling the con-
flicts outlined above. It must have a solid basis
of procedure. It cannot be superficial, *dilettante*,
or trivial in its aim or work. It must strike deep
into the constitution, nature, and possibilities of
the soul. It must be able to take a strong hold
on life, turn class and class to the appointed rank
and place of each, revolutionize and develop the
relations of men and women, build up right ideas,
grand affections, noble friendships and homes
among them; and it must take away from the
heart the spirit of insurrection and rebellion which
has kept it in antagonism to the decrees of God.
This is a large work.

To carry it through, reform must be adequate
to deal with the mysteries and powers of life.
There are thoughtful men and women who say:
All about me is mystery I can see but a step of
my way. I am incompetent for this strange life
which I am obliged to live. I need to know
higher things and reasons than I to-day have
grasped. I feel that I daily work with the Unknown — that it is guiding me, I know not how;
developing me, I know not for what; hurrying
me, I know not whither. This Unknown is more
real to me than anything I can hear, touch, or see.
Out of mystery was I born, and to mystery do I

return. There is the mystery of heredity. We do not know what a vast force it is until we have met life. We find things in ourselves and others which take us by complete surprise. We thought we were acquainted with ourselves, when circumstances bring us before a stranger. Some one three generations back appears, overturns our plans, shocks our pride, and baffles our best efforts, — some one incased in our own personality, and working through our own wills. We and our friends do things that defy our usual standards, and antagonize our well-known moods. Where do these strange instincts, these unruly passions, yea, and these awakening and startling powers, come from? Reform must take hold of this mysterious force, and, like an X-ray, pierce the darkness of ancestral and oncoming life, and show the soul the shadowgraph of its past, and the firm outline of its future hope.

Growth is a mystery. What we are, we know; but what we shall be to-morrow, who can tell? Growth is something which escapes our complete control. It takes unthought-of direction, and lays hold of destinies that did not cross our minds.

Personality is a mystery, — inherent power. We have something about us of which ourselves are unconscious. In all our lives we never find out what it is. If we had ten thousand photographs of ourselves, taken at ten thousand different moments unawares, I doubt if we should understand ourselves much better. We do not know

how we look. We do not know how we behave.
And yet our looks and our behavior are making
or marring our lives. "The power of manners,"
says Emerson, "is incessant, — an element as
unconcealable as fire." We cannot all be trained
alike, nor think alike when we are trained. We
do something that proves magnetic or repellant,
and we do not know why. Friends rise up to
bless us whose love we never sought, and we
find foes whose anger we never wittingly aroused.
We speak, and our words have the opposite effect
from our intent. What is the relation of reform
to this unbidden power?

Reform must give a joyous incentive to living.
To live is a delight to the normal man. There is
something abnormal and wrong when this primitive instinct dies out. An appalling aspect of the
times is the mania for suicide. What lies behind
the deed? The man is crazy with poverty, sin,
sorrow, or despair. He thinks life is not worth
living. He cannot stand it another hour. What
guidance must such undisciplined lives receive
from reform? How shall he be taught? Who
will put strong arms about him, and say, It is
not yet time to make way with yourself. Let God
be the judge of your length of days. Is the world
but a madhouse for lost souls? Will a plunge
into eternity give you real relief? Is there no
thinking there? Is the voice of conscience
stilled? — Ah, no! We must hold out some
high aim which will tide a man over the hard

places in life, and keep him from despondency. We must tell him what life is for, and set him to eager and loving service, instead of letting him blow his brains out like the veriest coward in space.

Reform must put a man's right work in his hands, and teach him to do it well. The idle are the unhappy. The unskilful are the irresolute and sad.

Reform must provide for eternal needs. We crave eternity. This life is not enough. We ask far more than threescore years and ten. In that time we but begin. We ask not only for long life, — we ask for wisdom, joy, hope, and peace. What reform will stand if it does not provide these things? Reform must somehow fit the race for its majestic future, far outliving Time, — for years beyond years, and for cycles that shall know no end. Reform must adjust time and eternity, and build to-day on foundations that shall never fail. What shall this foundation be?

In times past reform has been founded on many a shifting sand. One is so-called science. By this term has until recently been understood what I should call half-science, or, in truth, one-millionth science. The word has meant natural laws and classifications of facts already found out. But we do not yet know the whole of Nature and her relations, nor shall we know this whole, in all probability, for a thousand ages yet to come. We must make use of science at every step in reform, so far as we have discovered its facts and laws;

for the universe is built on true science, the larger science, which is the intellectual and creative activity of the Maker of all things. If we **do** not, our walls will topple, being untrue to necessary direction and proportion. Let science be the plumb-line, the T-square, with which we work. But the foundation-stone of reform must be sought in that which lies behind science, — a sentient, ruling, and directing power. Even the larger science is not final. It involves a huge imagination and a will. Nature is not self-originating. She did not make life. She cannot create it to-day. Nature is not perpetual. Although no force is lost, although no atom disappears, unless there is somewhere eternal and living energy, all things in our material world may sometime come to a strange, cold, and awful pause. There will be neither voice, motion, nor sound. The universe will run down.

Another says, We will build our work on individual insight, — on great men. The true reformers are seers. Looking over the past life of the world, they have analyzed its conditions. Looking over the present, they understand its aspects. Looking over the future, they see in what manner yesterday, to-day, and forever must be adjusted, in order to have peace, joy, and justice in the world. Do they? Are there really such final seers among us? Do the prophets yet live? Which of us, or of our race, is altogether knowing? For answer, we have only to run back over the history of human lack of judgment, folly, and mistakes. We are somehow and sometime in the colossal wrong. There are sharp limitations to human insight. If we cannot conduct ourselves with wisdom in our own simple circumstances, how can we trust our crude powers, our inadequate intuitions, our rash conclusions, and our precipitous decisions to lead us through the sublime problem of redeeming a world from want, sin, care, grief, and woe?

Will socialism do? There are many who are crying to-day: Let us share all things! Then our goods will be common. No one will be hungry or poor, and the even conditions of the race will make possible an ideal world. That reform, again, is but a surface thing. It does not touch the heart of life. We are hungry in other ways than for lack of bread. We are naked in other ways than to be without coat or boots. Socialism does not provide the best for man. There are good things we cannot share. For instance, a man produces $5,000. He may divide that amount with any number of others. But how can he share with them his delight in his work, the personal growth and development he received in the doing of it, or his rank in the universe as a producer instead of a parasite? We must find some way which shares things that are not material, which affords a transfer-system from soul to soul of the best spiritual concepts, interests, and delights.

Ah, says some one, that is altruism. We share the other's life. We give him ours. That is the

final solution. — No; it is not. We cannot give
him our real life, as we shall see. He can in part
seize the surface polish of it, — the clean clothes,
the better house, the keener mind, the washed face
and hands, the more refined amusements, the hon-
est vote, — but he cannot take the everlasting It
which will make the thing endure. We all know
that the educated criminal is the worst one. He
cannot be made upright working from the outside
in. There is a fiery spirit working in the heart
for righteousness which he can neither take nor
feel, unless a grand and subtle change is wrought
in the inmost fibres of his being. Can altruism
work that change?

It is not that I would in any way discount the
work of altruism. It is nobly unselfish, and does
something. In many ways it does much. I think
no loving word or work was ever yet cast into the
universe and returned unto a man void. But
the altruistic spirit cannot permanently remake
the race. Human nature is too much for it. It
lacks the inner motive-power. The altruist is
powerless to bring about those deep reverbera-
tions and activities of spirit which the simplest
Christian teacher can set up.

The root-question in social pathology should be,
not how to make life easy and agreeable for those
who are in a crippled physical or moral state, not
how to pamper the degenerates and fatten them,
but how to rid life of the pauper and criminal
instincts, how to develop and maintain a magnifi-

cent balance of physical and moral powers, which shall take away insanity, idiocy, feeble-mindedness, tramp-ways, and criminal passions, to a degree at least, from the earth. Will environment lastingly do this? Will new laws of marriage, liquor, and divorce? Will airy jails and penitentiaries? Will diet-schemes or potato-patches in themselves? Will even college settlements alone? "There is in man a Higher" than altruism or hygiene.

True reform strikes to the roots of life, and says, The first thing, O child of man! is to put this restless, angered, weary will of thine in harmony with the Divine Will. — Then all on earth will be forever well. The human will asks to indulge the senses, and the vagaries of an idle and undisciplined heart and brain. Hence arise drunkenness, disease, dirt, strife, revellings, tyranny, lawlessness, moral and spiritual uproar, and all social evils. The Divine Will asks to free the spirit, purify the affections, and renew and strengthen the will of man.

All reforms, rightly organized, must run back, as I see life, to one root-principle of organization and action. It is this: "*Seek ye first the kingdom of God.*" We must seek, not our own ideas, not social good alone, not changed environment, not education, not sanitary conditions alone, not correction, manners, nor political insight for men; we must seek to bring the kingdom of righteousness into their hearts and lives. Then, in time, all other good things may be added by the wise **and** tireless methods of our day. When eternal life gets hold of a man, it will build him up in this life, as well as for that which is to come. It will make him a centre of farther regenerating power. It will cast out evil spirits, wrong-doing, oppression, greed, drunkenness, theft, squalor, and the horrors of tenements and slums. It fulfils our three conditions: it is adequate, efficient, and permanent. Processionals of gods and goddesses pass and disappear in the twilight of time. The old theogonies fail. Nothing provides the motive-power for this spiritual change, so far as I can yet learn, except the cross of Christ. Sublime in history, towering above all schemes and speculations, the emblem of the Christian faith stands for a spiritual force which has proved itself supreme.

II. WHAT CULTURE CAN DO FOR REFORM.

Let culture add its insight to reform. We need the dispassionate view. Find the principle involved in each suggestion. Life is not so blind and confused as we think. Movements and tendencies are not so dimly outlined after all. There are many varying aspects of reform, many policies come to light, but there is an underlying principle somewhere. When found, it is invariably single. Every right is atomically distinct from every other right. It can be separated from everything else whatever. Culture holds the analytic and discerning power.

Reform should be kept clear of greed, cant, and

compromise. The spiritual world is a world of convictions. Many people do nót realize this. They try to avoid conviction. They say they are on the fence. They do not know how awkward they look. There is neither truth nor dignity in their position. We do not carry this sham into our businesss life, nor into that of our affections. The will at each moment finds the necessity of definite choice. If a man owes us money, we want that money paid. If he tries to avoid the issue by compromise or by slippery ways, we say to him plainly, You are a dishonest man. If we ask for love, we do not wish the one we love to say, "There are two sides to every question. There are two sides to loving you; I cannot decide either way." When we stop a trolley car, we do not sigh, " I cannot decide either to get out, or not to get out." If we pause even a moment in our decision, the conductor calls out, "Hurry up there!" He is running on time, and dare not be delayed.

Well, the world is running on time. The universe is running on time. The soul of man is running on time. Whenever we stop short of a decision when a square issue is before us, we delay the moral progress of the world; and God, looking down from heaven, sees that we are out of line with his.purpose and decree. Every duty before us is the eternal call, " Hurry up there, O halting soul of man ! "

We cannot, if we would, remain long in an ir-resolute position ; we shall be forced to one side or the other. The use of culture is to train the soul to prompt and right conviction. It is to give it such insight that it can pierce through sophistry and pretence, and arrive at clear-cut, definite convictions on issues that involve right and wrong. In order to have such convictions, personal sin must be cast out. The basis of uneasiness and irresolution is often some sin which a man or a nation will not give up. Each of us should take a stand. This does not mean that we should jump blindly into convictions just for the sake of having a fixed position ; it means that we should take into account the pro and con of each successive question before us, weigh our evidence, balance it against eternal principles, then make a firm decision, and stand by it, come life, come death !

Let the ruling dynasty be a Christian power. By dynasty I mean Common Councils, School Directors, Aldermen, Commissioners, Senators, Representatives, Mayors, Presidents, Diplomats, and Kings, — all who stand in the attitude of authority and judgment. A man's vote is a political mandate issued for or against the Christian state. His influence is a social imperator. Let them be given only for men who stand for upright Christian character. Will not this in time greatly lessen political spoils, corruption, and abuse of public trust?

Every act of legislation should assert a phase of moral law. How this decree would revolutionize our parliamentary action ! The question we should ask in regard to each reform bill is this :

Is it based on fundamental righteousness? Let us always imagine God the final lawmaker, and ourselves as merely trying to put on legal record his thought for the race. This will dispose at once of certain so-called reform measures just now in debate. For instance, would we conceive that society could be purified by moving a disorderly house from one street to another? Would we presume to take away the appetite for drink in a man by raising the license-fee of the man who sells it to him? Would we think to remove the curse from his heart by detailing the government to distribute drams?

Hold a moment! you cry. — Would you not rather have half a loaf than none at all? Would you not rather pass a half-measure than none, if the whole straightforward right measure is impossible, owing to the blindness, prejudice, cowardice, or crookedness of men? — No, I say. In the realm of morals there are no half-loaves. It is either bread or not bread at all. A proposed measure is either right, or it is not. If it falls in the not-right category, it can never prove a true basis of reform. If a cannibal is going to roast and eat a man, what difference does it make to rule that he shall roast and eat but half the man?

Some one urges, But the world will never be reformed if we proceed only along the path of what seems to us absolute right. It would take forever to do anything. We must conciliate, inch along, do the best we can by patching up a plausible something for the present. — No, again I say. We are not required to reform the world within a fixed time. We are given the two broad outlooks, — To-day and Forever. Our act of to-day should stand in the judgment of that final court of appeal. Speed is not the moral need; it is fidelity to truth.

Let the Bible be a universal text-book in the schools. How little real ethical teaching there is in our day! Children are growing up at random, without fixed moral standards. At home they are disobedient; abroad they are irreverent and un-abashed. Now, regardless of creed, I do not know any book which can be given to children, so terse, so simple, so strong, and so spiritually upbuilding as the Word of God. What a child learns before twelve years of age makes an indelible impress on his soul. For that reason I think he should have daily in his hand the great moral ideals of the race. I think he should recite, not only upon geography and grammar, but upon the principles of justice, honor, truth, mercy, charity, patience, courage, and forgiveness, which should underlie our private and our national life. Would not civic virtue thereby strengthen and increase?

Let culture care more kindly for the home. I do not know what is to become of our homes if the present conditions remain. Home-life seems to be taking to its heels. Clubs, inordinate travel, differing domestic ideas, and outside engagements are fast chasing it away. This cannot continue without grave social decline. They have their rightful place, but a new adjustment of all such claims must soon be made. If I could rearrange the curriculum of our colleges, university extension centres, Chautauqua circles, and other catholic movements, I would add whole courses of study on the things of home. I would have books and talks on friendship, marriage, social aims, and in-door ideals, which I think would help young men and women to realize more fully the possible solemnity, tenderness, and depth of life.

Let the Sabbath be remembered. If from the heart we try to keep it holy, using its grave, precious hours for worship, mercy, and need, we shall not fritter time and patience by asking, May we have Sunday beer? Sunday concerts and excursions? a Sunday press?

Let culture work grandly to build up the Christian church. No reform society should antagonize it. One of the most serious aspects of the times is the alienation of energy from the church. Other organizations, — social, benevolent, æsthetic, civic, and political, — each good in its way, are drawing away our spiritual force. Compare for preparation, variety, interest, and intellectual grasp the meetings of such organizations with the average weekday meetings of the church. Is this right? Is it just to God? Is there not something fundamentally wrong with the direction of our powers?

I am far from saying that every reform society should be, by formal alliance, a part of the church.

I am far from saying that the leaders of the church should be required to do double duty. I do say that the church is the one large social body which is distinctly divinely organized and sanctioned as an agent to preserve righteousness in the world. Its claim is definite, and stands first. We dare not ignore that claim, turn our backs upon it, and cry out pettishly in reform, We will not work with the church. It is too conservative! It is too old-fogy! It does not know what is going on in the world! Its head is under the hymn-book rack! — The great rescue-and-relief work of the world should start straight from the church. It may then be extended and built up by outlying societies which can best carry on specific details and phases of reform.

Primary stress should be laid upon missions. We speak of navigators, discoverers, and explorers with honor; but the real world-hero is the man like Livingstone, who has transformed a continent, or like Paton, who has made of man-eating savages a Christian state, and has replaced the fumes of cannibal feasts with the incense of family prayer.

Let culture guard the freedom, wages, and housing of each class. There is something wrong with our educational system if our women-teachers are so often tired. They should have less work, more society, and shorter hours. A teacher is of large economic value to the State, but her economic value decreases the moment she is over-worked or over-tired. She cannot give out inspiration; her fatigue does lasting harm. Every condition that preserves a teacher's strength, that cheers her heart, and that gives her life wide interests, adds ideals, brain-power, and possible prosperity to the land.

There is something wrong with our industrial system if it hampers a man's intellectual and spiritual freedom in any way. All right manual labor is spiritually free. Why should the spirit working through the hand of man be more constrained than that working through his tongue, heart, or brain? Wherever right conditions for work exist, the work itself may be made spiritual. I have seen righteousness exalted in a laundry and in machine-shops. Any system or environment which crushes a man into a machine or slave is a wicked one. It is the part of culture to remove the mechanical pressure on the lives of working-men and working-women, and give them their free souls back again. This is, in part, the meaning of industrial schools, and of all right working-homes. It is the meaning of the growing demand for hand-finished work. The fault of to-day is not that we use machinery. Machinery spares the soul. It knocks off the rough work of the world, and saves millions of years and untold volts of energy to the race. But after machinery has done its best, there should be added to work the living touch of love and human skill. We should have hand-work on nearly every simple thing we own and use. The worker then becomes a maker. The mutterings of industrial discontent begin to die away.

There is a certain wage — different for each man, it may be — beneath which he and his wife and children cannot live. There is a certain average sum for each class. The culture-world dare not stand by and let the industrial world look out for itself. To allow whole classes and districts of men or women to be crushed into semi-starvation or dishonor is an infamy to an age. Not less disgraceful to us are the squalid homes in which so many poor are forced to live.

If this freedom of spirit, wage, and shelter be denied, if workers are held down to a meaningless monotony of toil, machine-belts, bars, needles, and steam or electric pressure, there will be trouble. Just as surely as any class is held down, it will some day rise up, burst the withes about it, strike, and strike hard. Nature permits no lasting wrong to her children. Sooner or later each oppressed class, mediæval peasant, mill-operative, tailor, or coal-digger, asserts a right to this larger freedom.

Let culture add sense, manners, prestige, persistence, and trained wisdom to reform. There are too many reformers who have right ideas, but unbalanced ways. They are heterogeneous. They lack judgment and reserve. They are impulsive, eccentric, and tyrannical in outlook; and they drag down, in the eyes of rational people, the cause which they would help. Just here the trained powers of culture should come into play. Instead of saying, I will not work with such cranks! the man of understanding should say, Sense is my peculiar gift. It is what God has given me to work with in the world. I will add plain common-sense to the work of reform. Oh, if all the men and women of clear heads and good judgment would come into reform-work, what a millennium there would be!

It does not help a movement to be presumptuous, dictatorial, impertinent, or downright rude. Because others do not agree with our ideas, or find it possible to join us in our own work, we have no right to brand them loudly as shirks or cowards. Each man knows his own duty best. To try to map it out for him is to break a fundamental law. Into reform-work should be carried every charm of dress, look, and manner. Sometimes those who cannot be convinced by papers or argument are won over to a reform-cause by simple human charm. Reform is something which calls for a large amount of social tact. It demands etiquette. It goes so directly against the prejudices and sins of the world that it dare not be left without the help of gracious ways.

Whatever there is in your birth, rank, family name, honors, talent, or influence, put it all in: prestige is a most helpful ally of reform. As to persistence, the difference between untrained and trained energy is that the former relaxes. It blazes up like a fierce flare, and then dies out, while the other burns on like the lamps perpetual of Rome.

Culture affords the necessary intellectual preparation for the solution of great problems. Culture

CPSIA information can be obtained
at www.ICGtesting.com
Printed in the USA
BVHW041321151218
535629BV00023BA/1212/P

9 780259 292616